Growing in Communication

Living from your authentic power

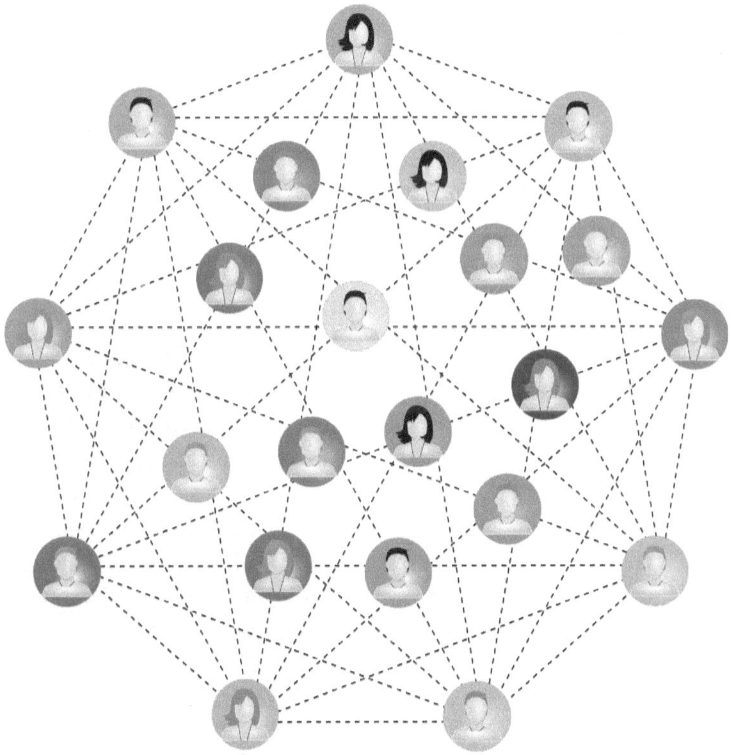

Alex Peeters & Marleen Devisch

Original title: **Groeien in communicatie**
Translators: **Marleen Devisch** & **Alex Peeters**
Author: **Marleen Devisch**
Co-author: **Alex Peeters**
Cover design & composer: **Alex Peeters**
ISBN: **979-83-2722-805-4** (paperback)
Publisher: GROEI ACADEMIE BV
Press-work: **Amazon**
Edition: 2ᵉ **print**
© 2024-2026 GROEI ACADEMIE BV, Marleen Devisch & Alex Peeters

All rights reserved by Alex Peeters & **Marleen Devisch,** GROEI ACADEMIE BV. No part of this publication may be reproduced and/or made public by means of print, photocopy, microfilm, internet or in any other way and/or by any medium without permission of both authors! You may not ask for/earn money based on this work without permission from both authors!

We have done our best to be as accurate and clear as possible. How you interpret the information offered is your responsibility.

Should you find errors in this book of any kind, please provide us with your feedback. Some of what we have written down here we have learned, read, unconsciously absorbed, borrowed or copied ourselves from someone else who is much smarter than us and/or who in turn has also learned it from others. No one needs to reinvent the wheel to be successful. We can embellish that wheel, imitate it, give it status, add our own input to it. That's called 'innovating'. Innovating is the most powerful way to be successful and to grow as human beings and as a human species.

https://groeiacademie.be

Inhoudsopgave

About the authors..5
Foreword..7
Introduction..9
1: Communicating: Connecting with the Other......................11
2: The foundation of connective communication....................13
   2.1: A few basic assumptions..15
   2.2: Learning to attune yourself to the other person........19
   2.3: What about the other person?...............................23
      2.3.1: Who is that other person anyway?.................23
      2.3.2: How does the other person think and feel?....25
      2.3.3: The needs of the other...................................31
   2.4: Really listening..35
3: What could go wrong?..37
   3.1: The true source of tensions and conflicts................39
      3.1.1: The 'inside' of conflicts.................................40
      3.1.2: Dealing with conflict.....................................43
      3.1.3: Pitfalls in seeking solutions............................45
      3.1.4: Take Realistic Steps.......................................46
      3.1.5: It is better not to avoid conflict......................46
      3.1.6: What you don't solve, you will certainly come across..........47
      3.1.7: Every conflict is an opportunity for growth....47
   3.2: Overreactions...51
   3.3: Infinite Needs..55
   3.4: No reception..59
   3.5: Cutting off the communication..............................61
   3.6 Hidden agendas...63
   3.7: To interpret...65
   3.8: Thinking Leaps..67
   3.9: Limiting words..69
   3.10: Getting old cows out of the canal.......................71
   3.11: Making incorrect connections.............................73
   3.12: To be vague..75
   3.13: Interrupt..77
   3.14: Too much attention for yourself.........................79
4: How could it be different?..81
5: Human-to-human encounter..85
Finally..87
Afterword..89
GROEI ACADEMIE...91
The Society of NLP...92

About the authors

Marleen & Alex help people change their lives so that they spend more time feeling good than feeling bad. In short, they help people on their way to maximum quality of life, happiness and success.

We build our own prison of thought. Only to be unhappy because we think that way. We twist ourselves into it. This causes great unfreedom in our lives.

Marleen & Alex work with NLP (Neuro-Linguistic Programming) so that they can gently move towards a life where other thoughts and feelings come to the foreground. More freedom, joy and impact are the result and so is a different way of life.

Alex Peeters & Marleen Devisch

Marleen & Alex have been business partners in addition to life partners since October 2013. They are both directors of GROEI *ACADEMIE BV*

Marleen Devisch, NLP Trainer™, NLP Coaching Trainer™, NLP Coach™ and mentor at GROEI **ACADEMIE**, life partner of Alex, has been active within personal development for over a quarter of a century. She understands the art of creating a climate of growth for people. Her great all-round experience with and understanding of people, makes her an indispensable supporter for anyone who follows training. She specializes in getting people in touch with the core of their personality and with their inner motivators. The calmness and simplicity of her approach and her enthusiasm are very inspiring and get people moving.

Alex Peeters, NLP Trainer™, NLP Coaching Trainer™, NLP Coach™ and mentor at GROEI *ACADEMIE, is the textbook example of what transformation someone at* GROEI *ACADEMIE can go through. Several years ago, he was diagnosed with autism. Hardly anyone believed he could become a trainer. Now he is an expert in business NLP training. He puts his autism to full use as a strength, so with his precision and sharp observations, he lifts people to an above-average level in their growth process. At* GROEI *ACADEMIE, he is the creator of many trainings. He is behind most of the books published by* GROEI *ACADEMIE. His passion for human growth is contagious.*

Foreword

You have chosen this book!

It is a powerful formula to start your growth process.

You can read this book several times and re-read it as often as you want and need it.

You can let it sink in for a while and then pick it up again.

You can engage with it at a time that suits you.

You don't need to move for it.

And above all: **you can get started with the many exercises that are contained in this book.**

Growing isn't just about gaining insight into yourself. It is also – and above all – applying these insights to your concrete daily life. **Every time you give yourself an experience, you also give yourself a present!** Because to experience is to do, to do is to learn, and to learn is to grow.

We, therefore, want to encourage you to practice and to repeat the material of this book until you have fully integrated it.

Marleen Devisch & Alex Peeters

Licensed Trainers of Neuro-Linguistic Programming®

Licensed Coaching Trainers of Neuro-Linguistic Programming®

Introduction

Much has already been saying and written about communication. It is therefore the basis of human contact. It's the 'cornflour' that connects people. It's an art we can spend a lifetime doing.

"You cannot, not communicate". Truth as a cow. There is always and everywhere communication, verbal and non-verbal. Many problems can be traced back to inadequate communication between people. Reasons enough for us to delve into it.

We offer you some unique tools that you can use, both in your personal life and in your professional relationships.

Learning to communicate is only possible through practice. You can immediately apply all the coat racks from this book in the reality of your daily life. Only through practice and repetition does it become yours and integrate it into your personality and your relationship life.

Take a deep dive into this book and allow plenty of time to complete all the exercises. Then you get a maximum result! And above all: **enjoy it!**

Thank you for allowing us to share our rich experience with you!

Marleen Devisch & Alex Peeters

Licensed Trainers of Neuro-Linguistic Programming®

Licensed Coaching Trainers of Neuro-Linguistic Programming®

1: Communicating: Connecting with the Other

Communication is connecting yourself with someone else. We are social beings, made to weave threads with other people. We were made to connect with the others.

The possibilities that we as human beings carry within us want to express ourselves. We want to shape them. We have desires and dreams. And we want to do something with our capabilities. We want to have a goal to strive for. We want to love and be loved. And we have needs that we want to get fulfilled.

For all these reasons, there is an urge in every person to show themselves to the outside world. And for that, communication is the binding agent. People grow in relationships with others and with the world. And without communication, that relationship is not possible.

2: The foundation of connective communication

There is communication that helps us to connect with others. There is also communication that drives us away from each other.

What is needed to establish connective communication?

We will take in a moment a dive into the basics of connective communication!a

2.1: A few basic assumptions

Communication requires a lot of skills. Many misunderstandings in communication arise from the fact that we do not understand the other person and/or ourselves enough.

Communication can go a lot smoother if we assume a few things in advance:

- **Each person has a certain view of themselves, others, the world.**

    Respect that image, that model of the world. Move into it. And know that a person will only accept your input in the communication if he feels understood and accepted in his view of things. Respecting this doesn't mean you have to agree with what the other person thinks.

- **When you communicate with others, you want to be understood yourself.**

If you don't get the response you expected, make sure you communicate it differently, until the other person understands. And based on the response you receive to your communications, you will know whether you need to adjust it or not.

- **When the other person has resistance, you better tune in to that person.**

Resistance on the part of the other does not just happen. Our communication may have touched a sensitive chord, maybe threatening to the other, maybe a big mirror to the other. Too much resistance means that your message does not get through and that you have not reached your goal. And the better you attune yourself to the other person, the more likely that what you want to convey will land.

- **Look through the other person's behavior.**

    People are more than their behavior. Behind every behavior is a person who strives for something, who wants to achieve something. And when you look through the behavior, you notice that the intention is often good.

- **Criticism is feedback.**

    Allow criticism from others as something you can learn from, not as an attack on your person. That is not always easy, because criticism affects us. If you are criticized, release the initial emotional charge within yourself. Give it some time, don't keep spinning in it. And ask yourself the question as soon as possible: "what can I learn from this?"

Exercise

- can you agree with the above basic assumptions?
- do you have a view of the model of the world that the people you communicate with have?
- if others feel misunderstood or show resistance, what do you do? What do you achieve with your way of doing things?
- can you see through people's behavior and see the person they are? How difficult or how easy is that for you?
- how do you receive criticism? What are you doing with it?

→ DO THE ABOVE EXERCISE NOW!

2.2: Learning to attune yourself to the other person

Communicating with others is much more likely to succeed if you tune in to the other person. Use all your five senses for this. Look at the other person. Watch his body language, his face, his eyes, his breathing. And adjust your body language, your voice, your speaking accordingly.

Listen to what he says. What words is he using? Does he speak fast or slow? Does he use many words, few words? And feel what the other person does to you.

Crawl into his world. Learn to understand his feelings. Take in every possible detail. Breathe along to the breathing rhythm of the other person. Tune in to the movements of the other person. Be calm when the other person is. Be mobile when the other person is mobile. And so on. That doesn't mean you have to make the same movements as the other, of course. And just tune in to his rhythm.

Tuning in to all possible facets of the other will give the latter security and a feeling of being understood. It's an important foundation for building trust. It requires that you put your focus on the other person and not on yourself. It asks that you put the other person in the foreground, in the first instance. And after that, your conversation partner will be much more willing to receive any difficult message.

Exercise

- practice this 'alignment' as much as you can, in any communication;
- regularly write down your findings: what comes easy to you? What are you having trouble with?
- what do you learn from all of this?

→ DO THE ABOVE EXERCISE NOW!

2.3: What about the other person?

Learning to tune in to the other person means that you enter his world. It means that you are confronted with a human being who thinks and feels, who has strengths and weaknesses.

What can you focus on?

2.3.1: Who is that other person anyway?

First of all, it's important to get in touch with the core of someone's personality. Who is that person? What are the positive intentions of that person? What are his capacities, dreams, desires? What does he aspire to? What are his beautiful sides? What positive facets do you see in him? Which good intentions? And where's its authentic side?

Exercise
- observe others: discover their strengths, the beauty in who they are, the authenticity in them. Write it down;
- what does it do to you to initially focus on that side of this person?
- what does it do with the communication you have?

→ DO THE ABOVE EXERCISE NOW!

2.3.2: How does the other person think and feel?

The other person not only has an authentic side. He is thinking and feeling. He has built certain strategies and systems for taking in and interacting with the world. And the better you know these systems, the better you can understand the other person and conduct your communication in such a way that the other person understands you too.

Many communication problems start from a lack of understanding of the way of thinking of the other person. And wanting to get someone into a frame of mind that is not his own will usually lead to resistance or misunderstanding.

Which systems can you keep an eye on?

- **Some people are oriented to what they want, others to what they don't want.**

    If you want to achieve something, with someone who is focused on what they want, then you can easily work towards a goal and all that he will have, when he achieves it. With such a person it is better to outline the advantages. And you will get someone who is focused on what he does not want, by telling him which negative things will no longer be there if he goes along towards a certain goal.

- **Some people mainly see similarities, others mainly differences.**

    When you want to get something done from them, when you want to get them to try something new, for example, you will get much more results if you point out to one how much of that new is the same as in the old, the other you will especially get when you highlight the difference with the old.

- **Some always need confirmation or a sounding board to know whether they are doing the right thing, others don't.**

  Don't force people who are team players by nature to go solo or vice versa. Find a middle way here.

- **Some only take action when they are forced to, others see possibilities and start on it.**

  So the one will need a stick and act only out of necessity, with others you just have to give them a push, and they are already in the action.

- **Some need an overview of something before they want to go into detail. And others want first to be able to see and grasp the details before they require a global view.**

  Your message will be best received if you give them what they need within their thinking system.

- **Some people always need to have choices, and they don't like being pushed into a take** or leave the structure. And others just need structure.

Depending on what the communication is about and what position you are in with them, this can be important. In raising children, for example, it can make a difference day and night if you realize that system in your child.

- **Some people like the abstract, and others are concrete thinkers and need examples before understanding anything.**

While some will be annoyed by practical examples, others will need them just to understand what it is about.

- **And so on.**

There are many such systems of thought. We've listed a few to get you started. The point is that you learn to understand those systems in others so that you can tailor your communication to them. Many people tend to impose their thinking systems on others. Or one system is assigned a higher value than the other. And no thought system is good or bad, better or less good than another. Get to know your communication partner and have your message packaged in such a way that he or she can recognize it and let it in.

Exercise

- observe others: find out their thinking systems. Map them out,
- package your communication in such a way that it is embedded in the thinking systems of the other person,
- what does it do with the communication you have?

→ DO THE ABOVE EXERCISE NOW!

2.3.3: The needs of the other

Every person has abilities. Everyone thinks and feels in their way. Every human being has needs. That's normal. And a desire is a movement from the inside out. We want to express something about ourselves. And a need, on the other hand, is a movement from outside to inside. We want to have something.

Every person has a normal need for attention, recognition, understanding, love, being seen, appreciation, opportunities, and so on. If this need is not met or not fully met, we feel that frustration, but we can live with it for a while. We don't lose our balance. And we have sufficient capacity to handle those frustrations.

However, some needs are like a bottomless barrel. No matter how much you pour in, it's never enough. Sometimes you get people who constantly demand all the attention, in the most annoying ways. Others are constantly focused on recognition and appreciation. And still, others are constantly looking for love, in all kinds of compensations.

When a need that is present in someone like a bottomless barrel is frustrated, then that person can hardly bear the frustration. Usually, an entire system starts to work, causing the person to search for fulfillment of that need in a compelling and often convulsive way. And so someone can start exhibiting stalking behavior, send a lot of emails, become very dependent, constantly want to be noticed, and so on.

These "bottomless vessels" usually have their roots in childhood. When a child is insufficiently seen or hurt in certain needs, that need installs itself like a bottomless barrel. And as adults, we continue to search for its meaning.

In communication, we must learn to recognize these bottomless vessels, both in ourselves and in others. And it helps to keep our communication in proper proportions.

Exercise

- do you recognize in yourself the difference between healthy needs and needs that resemble a bottomless barrel?
- what happens if an 'excessive' need is not fulfilled or not fulfilled enough?
- how do you then communicate?
- do you recognize this in other people?
- how do you communicate with them?

→ DO THE ABOVE EXERCISE NOW!

2.4: Really listening

Many of us think we can listen. When we practice this in training, people notice that they often don't listen at all. Genuine listening takes effort. It takes that you want to understand the other person. It takes patience to let the other person finish speaking. If you listen, you have your attention to the other person and not on what you want to say yourself. And your focus is on the person in front of you and on the respect for who this person is.

Exercise

- what does real listening mean to you?
- what listening skills do you have?
- what else can you work on to become better at listening?

→ DO THE ABOVE EXERCISE NOW!

3: What could go wrong?

Anything can go wrong in communication. However, sometimes it all seems much worse than it is and with a few minor interventions, you can get the communication going again.

3.1: The true source of tensions and conflicts

Tensions and conflicts are not the same things.

Tensions are very normal, they occur in any situation where people are brought together. And when you recognize tensions and deal with them promptly on time, they don't have to become conflicts.

Conflicts are, in fact, unresolved tensions. And often they come gradually into existence and burst open at some point.

Conflicts don't just happen. They are caused by a variety of factors.

There is the 'outside' of a conflict: 'the facts, the situation...'. And there is the 'inside' of a conflict: 'the causes, which can lie in yourself, in the other person, as well as in the situation itself'.

3.1.1: The 'inside' of conflicts

It is very tempting to stick to the facts when looking for how to deal with a conflict. But to find a real solution, you have to keep looking.

Not only looking at 'what are the facts, what is the situation', but especially at: 'how do I experience those facts?' We often tend to put everything outside us: it is the others, the circumstances, and so on. And when those others would change, everything would be solved...

However, when we look very honestly, we often discover a different story. Every person is full of desires: 'we want to shape things, we want to express ourselves, we want to offer people something, we want to develop our capabilities'. When that natural drive in us is hindered, it can lead to conflict. For example, if you are a very communicative person who likes to be open-minded and your partner keeps rejecting communication or finds that openness threatening, then you become deeply frustrated in your capacity to communicate. And that could lead to conflict.

As we saw before, we also have needs: we need attention, respect, confirmation... And that's normal. If you get no or an insufficient answer to those needs and that for a long time, this can also lead to conflicts. And when you try your best all the time and never get a compliment in return, then a normal need in you isn't being answered. We can usually live with that for a while. But if the answer is delayed for too long, it can lead to difficulties.

The root causes of a conflict can usually be traced back to these two movements in us: something you want will not get an opportunity and/or something you need will not receive an answer.

All this does not mean that you should only look for every cause of conflict within yourself. Where the causes can be located in several areas:

- **Within yourself:** when you discover that, you have to take responsibility for it: by speaking, by letting you help, by learning to look more objectively, by learning to let go...

- **Within the other:** when you see that the cause lies in the other, then you should leave it there. You cannot change the other person, no matter how much you would like to. If you have difficulty with that, then it is good to look inside yourself to see what is difficult for you and to see if and how you can learn to deal with that other person differently.

- **The cause can also lie with third parties, in the situation itself:** 'then it is good to discuss it together with the parties involved, to do something about it together if possible, to let time pass...'

3.1.2: Dealing with conflict

We all have our way of dealing with conflict. How we do that depends on many factors.

You can run away from conflict. You can stiffen. You can go into battle. You can blame the other. You can cover everything with the cloak of love. And you can be authoritarian. But you can also start looking constructively for the causes and from there for solutions.

Finding solutions to a conflict always means facing what is going on. It also means that you have to start the conversation with the other person. It means searching in a realistic and often creative way for realistic steps that you can take now, today. And that usually won't solve the conflict in one go, but it will open the way for it to grow towards a solution.

It is bad for you to be tempted into a power game. There is always a winner and a loser, always someone who is right and someone who loses. That is the worst possible option. And if you want to be right, you can check with yourself why you want that, what the reason is.

A conflict is something that we are in between with our 'skin'. It's a minefield, and if we stay in the middle of it, there's little chance we'll come up with a good solution.

That is why it is very important to distance yourself. Distancing yourself is not the same as isolating yourself and waiting passively. It does mean: 'Step out of that minefield, take a step back, wait a little while until things have calmed down a bit, and you can think, wait until you can fall back on your strength, on your patience, on the fact that you can other likes, and so on'. As a result, the perspective with which you look at the conflict changes becomes more objective, less emotional. You will look at things more within the right proportions and that is necessary to arrive at a solution. So don't look for a solution when you're emotionally still at a loss.

In seeking solutions, you should also be aware of past experiences that play a role in the conflict: 'you may have experienced similar things in the recent or more distant past, which can make you hypersensitive in the present. Or a previous conflict with the same person has not yet been digested and thus still hangs between you and the other'. And that is extra 'fuel' for the current conflict.

Looking for solutions to a conflict also means 'being alert for traps'.

3.1.3: Pitfalls in seeking solutions

There are a lot of them. And most importantly, get to know your traps!

Shut up, pretend everything is ok, fly out, overeat, run away, remain silent (image without sound), lock yourself in stubbornness, work too much, take it out on others, can no longer sleep, generalize, dramatize (the words 'always' and 'never' are signallers here), lingering in the emotional, not wanting to face what is going on, getting old cows out of the ditch, blaming and insulting the other and using disrespectful language, reacting from ingrained principles (men are all the same...), filling in what the other thinks...

3.1.4: Take Realistic Steps

Resolving a conflict often involves a multistep plan. Sometimes it's a complicated mess. You must look at which step is now feasible: 'what makes sense? And what will you and the other person do good and give oxygen again?'

You may protest a bit emotionally at such a step. Because maybe you want to be right, or maybe the solution you had in mind is not quite what has come out. That can cause frustrations. But if you then look at the whole in all its parts, so to speak, then you can see that, despite the frustrations you feel, you can still take the right step. It's a big trap to think that a solution to a conflict always makes you feel completely good. And that is rarely the case!

3.1.5: It is better not to avoid conflict

First, 'you really can't do this'. And conflicts can also play a very subcutaneous role and are then like a poison that does its job anyway.

It would be too easy to say, 'whoever avoids conflict does so out of fear of not being good enough, out of fear of not being liked'. Of course, those things can play a role. But the reality is that you have to see what is going on with each person individually, it is different for everyone. So it is important that people learn to look within themselves, that they learn to analyze their experience. This way you can do a lot of work yourself and avoid a lot of difficulties!

3.1.6: What you don't solve, you will certainly come across

You can run away from business for a long time, but sooner or later you will be presented with them. Here too: 'learn to see what's going on'. And then you don't have to make so many detours.

3.1.7: Every conflict is an opportunity for growth

Conflicts are not pleasant and we should not go looking for them, we do not need them to move forward. But if they are there, we can learn to look at them as an opportunity to learn about ourselves, about who we are, to take steps in communication, in getting stronger, and so on. And so conflicts can be fruitful in the end!

Exercise
- what tensions are you dealing with?
- are there conflicts in your life?
- do these tensions or conflicts have to do with a desire that is given little or no chance?
- do they have to deal with one or more needs that are not fulfilled or not met enough?
- is the cause of the tension or conflict partly or completely with yourself, with the other person, with the situation? Take a very honest look at this;
- do past experiences play a role?
- can you empathize with the story and the experience of the other person who is dealing with this tension or conflict?
- what step could you take now in the direction of a solution?
- what traps to watch out for?

→ DO THE ABOVE EXERCISE NOW!

3.2: Overreactions

Sometimes it happens to us that our response to an event is disproportionate to what is going on. When someone parks his car in front of your garage, it is normal to get angry. However, when you start scolding for it and are still off the map three days later, something is wrong. When you walk around euphorically for days after a course that you have followed, something is not right either. And when you completely shut down after a critical remark from your director and are depressed for days, then it's not right either.

Such reactions are exaggerated. And it's as if the world is coming to an end when in reality there is often not much going on. However, we cannot put it into perspective. And this is a drama in every language!

What is the reason that we react so strongly or that he can shut down completely to something that givesus no reason at all?

We have all experienced things in our lives that have hurt us. Unprocessed pain is nestled somewhere inside us. It is usually encapsulated so that we do not suffer from it. Sometimes, however, a situation pierces through that encapsulation, causing us to feel that original pain again. We react as if we were stung by a bee. So, in other words, we are reacting to a past pain, which bears some resemblance to the present situation. It has nothing to do with the present. Where the present is only the trigger, not the cause!

Overreactions are very often the cause of arguments and conflicts. So, learn to recognize them!

Exercise

- do you recognize overreactions in yourself? Give some examples,
- of who or what usually triggers an overreaction in you?
- what exactly do you feel at the moment of the overreaction?
- what do you feel afterward, when the emotions have already subsided?
- which strengths in you don't get enough life chances if you stay in your emotions?
- do you recognize overreactions in others? Give some examples,
- how do you usually deal with other people's overreactions?
- what else would you like to learn to better deal with your overreactions and those of others?

→ DO THE ABOVE EXERCISE NOW!

3.3: Infinite Needs

We already talked about it: 'there are needs and needs'. Every person has needs. These needs require an interpretation, adapted to the age, the situation, the person. And the need for attention of a child, for example, requires a different answer than that of an adult.

When adults get frustrated with a normal need, it's not nice, but we can bear it for a while. And we have the strength for it!

A child, on the other hand, has not yet been able to build this strength. When a child receives during a long time no, insufficiently or inappropriate response to normal needs, an injury will be installed in this child. A child cannot handle this. And it does not yet have sufficient insight into the other, the situation and itself to be able to place the event.

It does not yet have enough capacity to absorb the frustration of not getting what it is entitled to. A child will fight to survive in such a situation, for example by playing the clown, by quietly and obediently withdrawing into a corner, by adapting very much to his environment to appreciate something, by rebelling violently, and so on. And these survival strategies are not enough to take the pain away, however.

This pain is encapsulated and sits there like a silent desire waiting for an answer. In this way, you see that people who suddenly do get attention in adulthood, start to react to it like a hungry child. And what they have encapsulated since childhood wakes up and for the time being, asks for interpretation.

The problem is that this isn't possible anymore. We can't be kids again. And we can't turn back time. This issue does not go away by going along with their needs indefinitely with these people. Because you can keep giving them attention, recognition, confirmation... it won't help. And it's a bottomless barrel.

It never gets filled in. People with infinite needs have to learn to face their pain. Understanding this system can already help you learn the difference between normal and exaggerated needs. When others dare to respond to their normal needs and not to their exaggerated needs, they are given the opportunity to get through that pain.

These mechanisms can be a major problem in communication. We sometimes see people give up, every time they get too frustrated with something they want. They do not see that it is a child's need and they continue to look for answers to something that can no longer be answered. We see aggression in some. We see people who clap at the slightest. Furthermore, we see people who put themselves in the victim role, to get attention.

And we see people building their lives around 'gaining recognition'.

The consequences of unrecognized childhood needs in an adult's life can be profound. It is an intense process to gain insight into that and to find a way to more mature behavior.

Exercise
- do you know people with infinite needs?
- how do you deal with the infinite needs of others?
- how do you deal with the infinite needs within yourself, if you have them?
- what else would you like to learn about this theme?

→ DO THE ABOVE EXERCISE NOW!

3.4: No reception

At times, our message seems to fall on deaf ears. Our communication partner is not attentive, is busy with other things, is not interested in what we have to say, does not answer, is defensive about our message, and so on. In other words, our communication doesn't land.

What to do with this?

First of all, it is important to consider why someone is not receptive to what we want to convey. Does our message come at the wrong time? Is it the wording? Isn't this person the right person to pass it on to?

There could be many reasons why there is "no reception". And at such moments we mustn't want to impose our communication at all costs.

Exercise

- give examples of communications in which you did not receive a 'reception',
- what did you do to get it?
- what was the outcome of this?
- do you ever find yourself refusing to receive communication from the other person?
- if so, then why is that?
- what usually happens if you don't receive the message?

→ DO THE ABOVE EXERCISE NOW!

3.5: Cutting off the communication

You have undoubtedly experienced it or done it yourself: 'you are talking to someone and the conversation is difficult'. And suddenly the other person stands up, leaves the room, with or without slamming doors. End of communication. Or the other person (or you) says something along the lines such as: 'Whatever you say, I'm right. Forget it. No matter what you try, you won't convince me.' And so forth.

People usually cut off communication out of powerlessness. They feel cornered, assaulted, hurt, threatened. There's a short circuit, one way or another, that makes them go on the defensive and cut off communication, as it were. And they're shutting down to further input, so to speak.

Most of the time it doesn't help to move them to something else at the moment. Waiting for a while, let it cool down a bit and when things have calmed down, taking up the thread again is usually the only way out.

Exercise

- do you recognize this phenomenon in yourself and/or others?
- if you cut off communication yourself, how do you get out of it?
- if someone else cuts off communication with you, what do you do to get the conversation going again?

→ DO THE ABOVE EXERCISE NOW!

3.6 Hidden agendas

Open communication has no double bottoms. Your goal should be clear to the other person. Having a conversation about theme x while secretly broaching theme y in the meantime does not inspire confidence in the other person. And eventually, they will wonder what's behind everything you say. So, be honest and straightforward.

Exercise

- which hidden agendas have you already experienced with others?
- do you sometimes have a hidden agenda and if so, which one?
- if you have a hidden agenda in communication, what is the reason for it?
- if you notice that someone else has a hidden agenda in communicating with you, how do you deal with it?

→ DO THE ABOVE EXERCISE NOW!

3.7: To interpret

It happens before we realize it: 'what we perceive with our senses, we interpret in our way'. Entering a room and noticing that the conversations have stalled quickly makes you think they were talking about you. And you are convinced that you are right, while you are not going to check your assumption. So, you don't know, while you are sure that what you think is true.

These thought twists are poison in communication. The difficulty is that we take our interpretations for granted and build our further communication on them. In the long run, you end up with a whole array of stories based on something that might be completely wrong.

And it is the basis of many fights and even feuds. In the long run, no one will know anymore what is true and what is not.

Exercise
- do you recognize this phenomenon?
- give some examples of how you interpreted information yourself, without checking whether it was true or not;
- give examples of other people's interpretations;
- how do you deal with other people who interpret things without checking them?
- how come you don't check your interpretations for their truthfulness?

→ DO THE ABOVE EXERCISE NOW!

3.8: Thinking Leaps

When we interact with others, they need to be able to follow our story. Sometimes we think for ourselves, and we travel a long way in our head, but we forget that others do not know what we have thought. And this can lead to funny situations, where someone suddenly starts talking about something and the environment is wide-eyed, because no one even remotely knows what it is about. So, keep in mind that others don't know what's going on inside your head.

Exercise

- do you think sometimes?
- do you know people who easily think leaps and bounds?
- how do you cope with that?

→ DO THE ABOVE EXERCISE NOW!

3.9: Limiting words

Some words tend to block communication: always, never, must... We use them to lock ourselves and others. And it is oversimplified language, which leaves no room for creativity, for new ways and solutions.

Exercise

- how often do you use the word 'should' when communicating with others?
- how often do you use words such as 'never', 'always'?
- to what extent do these words help the communication you conduct?
- how much do they hinder communication?

→ DO THE ABOVE EXERCISE NOW!

3.10: Getting old cows out of the canal

When you start communicating with someone, stick to the theme you want to talk about in the now. Don't drag the whole past into it. And don't bring up the same stories for the umpteenth time.

Some people seem to feel the need to keep rehashing the past. Usually, they have not processed certain things, and they are left with frustration, anger, sadness, bitterness, or any other emotion. And they want satisfaction for the time being. Learn to separate these unresolved feelings from the current communication you are having. And keep the now and the past separated.

Exercise
- do you easily get old cows out of the canal?
- how do you feel when someone else does this?
- how can you avoid having a conversation with someone bogged down because old cows are being taken out of the canal?

→ DO THE ABOVE EXERCISE NOW!

3.11: Making incorrect connections

We tie things together in our brains. Often those things have little to nothing to do with each other. 'The rain makes me depressed'. No, the rain makes you wet. And the rest you create yourself. What we identify as the cause is not always the real cause of our behavior or how we feel.

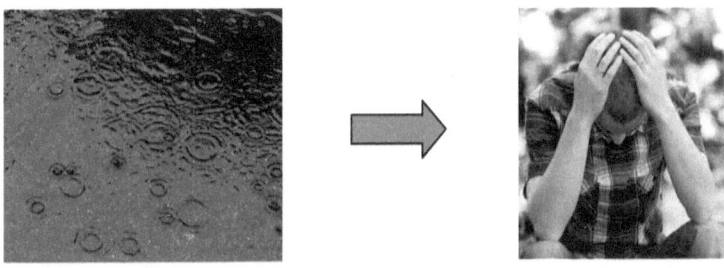

We are often convinced of this link between two things. Going against it won't take anyone out of their reasoning. And asking questions can make someone aware of the often nonsensical connections we make in our heads. Questions such as: 'how do you know? What makes that...?' can disprove someone's conviction to a significant extent.

Exercise
- find examples of statements (in yourself or others) in which someone makes incorrect connections,
- check whether you can bring about a change in that reasoning by asking the above questions.

→ DO THE ABOVE EXERCISE NOW!

3.12: To be vague

We are not always clear about what we communicate. Vague statements are open to many interpretations and often form the breeding ground for misunderstanding or irritation. Statements such as: 'they say that everyone, nobody...' is so vague that you can use them in many directions. Again, asking questions to help someone articulate things more precisely: 'who are they? Who? About what? When exactly? Where exactly?...' make communication clearer and more precise.

Exercise
- find examples of vague statements (in yourself or others),
- check whether you can make the communication clearer and more precise by asking the questions above.

→ DO THE ABOVE EXERCISE NOW!

3.13: Interrupt

Letting someone finish is a basic rule in any communication. Interrupting each time while someone is still fully articulating their point of view can be very irritating and interrupts the dynamics of the moment. And giving each other the space to fully express themselves brings peace and confidence to the conversation.

An exception to this rule occurs when someone wants to draw all the attention to themselves and want to speak constantly. In that case, it is often necessary for someone else to direct the communication a little more tightly. And that can be done in a very warm human way.

Exercise

- can you make people speak?
- how good are you at it?
- what difficulties do you encounter in getting someone to speak up?
- what does it do to you when others don't let you finish?
- how do you react if they don't let you finish?

→ DO THE ABOVE EXERCISE NOW!

3.14: Too much attention for yourself

Healthy communication requires a good balance between attention to yourself and attention to the other person. And a good conversation requires 'double attention': you are focused on the other person, you immerse yourself in the experience of the other person. At the same time, you are aware of what you feel and experience yourself.

Without this 'double attention', it is possible that you either neglect yourself too much and start ignoring your own experience, or that you are too busy with yourself and want to put yourself in the center of communication. The latter comes at the expense of the others. And people who are not very assertive will not dare to respond to this and remain in the shadow of the conversation or even drop out.

Exercise

- how do you experience the balance between attention for yourself and attention for the other person within the communication you conduct?
- can you easily use double attention in your communication?
- what can you do more/differently to be able to experience good double attention?

→ DO THE ABOVE EXERCISE NOW!

4: How could it be different?

Can it be done differently? Of course, there is another way! And below are some tips that can support you in your communication:

- **be open** to what communication entails. Don't predetermine everything. Let the moment do its work,

- **dare to ask questions.** If you don't understand something, if you want something more clear, if you want to find out something, ask. And often you benefit from the information that comes to the table through your questions,

- **do not judge too fast.** Do not put labels directly on the other person or on yourself. Let the dynamics of communication do their job. Give a communication time to emerge and to develop. And by judging you shut everything down and you and your conversation partner may miss valuable opportunities for conversation,

- **check whether your interpretations match reality.** So go and verify as much as possible. And this prevents your communication from being based on an untruth,

- **make your message clear and plain, and use nuanced language.** No black and white communication, no all or nothing words. And this will allow you to deepen and refine your communication greatly.

- **connect with others and with yourself.** Use that double attention to maintain a good balance between you and the other. And it prevents you from giving too much or too little space to the other person and from effacing yourself or drawing too much attention to yourself,

- **shows all possible respect for the other.** And don't pretend to have any respect,

- **make sure there is room to speak and to listen.** And start communication when you have time and if you can free your inner self for the other person,

- **leave room for the unexpected, for the moment itself.** Do not fill in the entire communication process beforehand,

- **trust in the first instance, the other.** Depart from that base,

- **don't be intent on trying to be right.** Wanting to equalize brings winners and losers. And strive for a win-win situation, so that all parties can feel good and that everyone has received minimum answers to essential needs and desires.

Exercise

- which of the above tips appeals to you most?
- what tips are you well on your way?
- around which tips do you feel you still have work?

→ DO THE ABOVE EXERCISE NOW!

5: Human-to-human encounter

Communication in the purest sense of the word focuses on 'encounter'. Meet the other in an authentic way, in all openness and honesty. It is a connection between the used part of two or more people, to come to real contact. And it's creating a framework that helps yourself and others to be yourself, to be authentic.

When this is the foundation of your communication, then a lot can be done. And not every moment of communication will be equally good or fruitful. But it will always be an opportunity for growth, for everyone who participates.

Exercise

- what do you want to grow in about concerning communication?
- what help do you need with this?
- what is the first step you can take to move forward?

→ DO THE ABOVE EXERCISE NOW!

Finally

We have come to the end of this book. You have been given a lot of tools, that you can use. And with these tools you can come a long way.

However, in our experience, people need a little more support when applying these tools. Or that they want to explore certain tools in more depth. And that is perfectly possible!

On our Dutch websites:
- https://www.groeiacademie.be/
- https://onlineleren.groeiacademie.be/

you will find many options to continue your journey!

Afterword

You have reached the end of this book!

Hopefully, you have been able to extract what is now useful for your growing process!

Maybe you're curious or hungry for more.

We have other books for you as well!

When we can be of service to you with anything, please let us know.

We are happy to assist you where we can!

Best of luck on your further growth path!

Marleen Devisch & Alex Peeters

Licensed Trainers of Neuro-Linguistic Programming®

Licensed Coaching Trainers of Neuro-Linguistic Programming®

NLP Communication Institute

Training Institute and Expertise Center for NLP licensed by the Society of NLP™

GROEI ACADEMIE BV

Katelijnestraat 116a
8000 BRUGGE

GSM
+32 50 94 68 43

E-Mail
info@groeiacademie.be

The Society of NLP™

GROEI ACADEMIE BV is affiliated with the international Society of Neuro Linguistic Programming™

GROEI ACADEMIE BV is recognized as an **NLP Training Institute in Belgium** by the international Society of Neuro Linguistic Programming™.

Alex Peeters and **Marleen Devisch** can be found both as **Licensed Trainer of NLP™** and as **Licensed Coaching Trainer of NLP™** in **Database of Licensed Trainers of Neuro-Linguistic Programming™**.

The Society of NLP™ founded by **Dr. Richard Bandler** in 1978, is the oldest and worldwide largest organization for NLP. It was founded for the purpose of exercising quality control over training programs and services representing the model of Neuro-Linguistic Programming (NLP™).

Dr. Richard Bandler and **John La Valle**, supported by **Kathleen La Valle**, are actively developing NLP and training new NLP Practitioners, NLP Master Practitioners, NLP Advanced Master Practitioners, NLP Trainers, NLP Coaching Trainers, ... The way Dr. Richard Bandler teaches NLP has evolved over the years to 'the simpler, the better'.

NLP Communication Institute

GROEI ACADEMIE, the NLP Communication Institute par excellence, with the most complete offer within Europe!

We teach how to use your brain, change your life, so that more energy and life dynamics are released, and you experience more happiness and successful acting!

Those who train with us choose trainers with a great deal of experience who teach you, "to 'Think' differently, to 'Communicate' differently to Influence with Impact, for a life with **Maximum Quality of Life & Success** in all areas of life!"

Our starting point is: "Every human being has a '**diamond**' in himself! Some are already partly polished, others are still quite rough. At GROEI ACADEMIE we provide an **NLP toolbox**, so that you can polish this diamond yourself, up to your desired level: beginner, advanced, advanced to expert!"

At GROEI ACADEMIE, we do what we do because we believe that everyone deserves Maximum Quality of Life and Success! We put our focus on the strengths and opportunities in people's differences, not their limitations. And we live what we teach to others. This is also our aspiration in all our trainings: "that what people learn there becomes a life attitude, your way of being."

The participants who find the greatest satisfaction with us are those who want a full-fledged NLP toolbox and who intend to go through the various levels from beginners, advanced, advanced to experts, with this toolbox. They do this in order to eventually become true experts in it, greatly enhancing and accelerating their professional & personal growth, making them much more effective, and with impact communicating & influencing, training, coaching, motivating, speaking to lifting themselves to another dimension!

Our NLP trainings include the levels: 'Practitioner, Master, Coach & Advanced', also the Business-levels. They are internationally recognized NLP trainings and courses by the 'Society of NLP™'. We train from experience: no theory or talking about, but a lot of doing, from the lived **CODEC model**!

So grant you our powerful **NLP toolbox** usable in the Workplace, in Daily Life, in Communication with people with autism and their environment.

Growing in Communication

Living from your authentic power

A lot has been said and written about communication. It is therefore the basis of the contact between people. It's an art we can spend a lifetime doing. "You cannot, not communicate". Truth as a cow. There is always and everywhere communication, verbal and non-verbal.

Many problems can be traced back to a lack of communication between people. This book provides you with unique tools for your private and professional life. Learning to communicate is only possible by practicing it. You can apply everything from this book directly to the reality of your daily life.

Marleen Devisch & **Alex Peeters**

Growing in Communication

Living from your authentic power

A lot has been said and written about communication. It is therefore the basis of the contact between people. It's an art we can spend a lifetime doing. "You cannot, not communicate". Truth as a cow. There is always and everywhere communication, verbal and non-verbal.

Many problems can be traced back to a lack of communication between people. This book provides you with unique tools for your private and professional life. Learning to communicate is only possible by practicing it. You can apply everything from this book directly to the reality of your daily life.

Marleen Devisch & Alex Peeters

www.ingramcontent.com/pod-product-compliance
Lightning Source LLC
Chambersburg PA
CBHW031447210526
45464CB00005B/2361